LOU HENRY HOOVER
The Duty To Serve

Notable Americans

LOU HENRY HOOVER
The Duty To Serve

Nancy A. Colbert

MORGAN
REYNOLDS
Incorporated

Greensboro

LOU HENRY HOOVER: *The Duty To Serve*

Copyright © 1998 by Nancy Colbert

Photo credits: Herbert Hoover Presidential Library—West Branch, Iowa.

Library of Congress Cataloging-in-Publication Data
Colbert, Nancy A.
  Lou Henry Hoover : the duty to serve/ Nancy A. Colbert.
  —1st ed.
      p. cm. — (Notable Americans)
  Includes bibliographical references and index.
  Summary: A biography of the wife of President Herbert Hoover, following her life from
birth to death.
    ISBN 1-883846-22-6 (hardcover)
        1. Hoover, Lou Henry, 1874-1944—Juvenile literature. 2. Presidents' spouses—
United States—Biography—Juvenile literature. 3. Hoover, Herbert, 1874-1964—Juvenile
literature. [1. Hoover, Lou Henry, 1974-1944. 2. First ladies. 3. Hoover, Herbert, 1874-
1964.] I. Title II. Series.
E802.1.C65   1997
973.91 '6' 092—dc21

                                                                    97-33329
                                                                    CIP

Printed in the United States of America
First Edition

*Dedicated with special thanks and love
to my husband, Jim, and to our children, Jim, and his wife,
Karen, and their children, James and Mikaela;
Susan, and her husband, Paul, and their daughter, Georgia
Anne; Sally, and her husband, Pat, and their children,
Jessica, Sean, Michael, and Mary Theresa;
Mary Ellen, and her special friend, Dwight;
Martin, and his son, Adam, and his special friend, Marijane.*

Many persons helped make this book possible. I'd especially like to thank the staff at the Herbert Hoover Presidential Library and Museum in West Branch, Iowa, particularly Dale C. Mayer, the Lou Henry Hoover expert archivist, who took his time to advise me and to read my manuscript; J. Patrick Wildenberg, archivist, who was never too busy to answer my many questions; Wade Slinde who graciously helped me with whatever I needed; Mary Evans, Education Programs Director, who gave me her encouragement; Jim Detlefsen, who looked up hundreds of pictures for me; and Cindy Worrell, who saw that I had all the research materials I would use.

Thank you to those who spent their time reading my work and giving words of advice: my husband, Jim; Mary; Sally; Jessica, and Mikki. Thanks also to Karen, an author comrade, who has been my sounding board. Thank you to everyone who encouraged me and helped me.

Contents

Lou Henry Hoover

Chapter One

Midwest Beginnings

When Lou Henry was five-years-old, her father began taking her fishing in his flat-bottomed boat on the Red Cedar River near their home in Waterloo, Iowa. She learned to tie penny-apiece fish hooks onto butcher string and then sit patiently beside her father, waiting for a fish to bite. She caught bullheads, or sometimes a catfish, and knew to watch out for their pokers.

Lou, a first child, was born on March 29, 1874. Her mother, Florence, taught school when her health allowed and her father, Charles Henry, ran the local bank.

Lou often visited Grandmother Mary Dwire Henry. Several other relatives lived nearby. Grandfather Phineas and Grandmother Philomel Weed lived in Shell Rock and Dr. John and Nancy Scobey, her great-grandparents, lived on a farm at the edge of Shell Rock. Lou specially loved Dr. John, with his white hair and full beard, and spent her vacations at his farm.

When Lou was six, Dr. John lifted her up on the broad back of the steady old farm horse and let her ride bareback. Later, her father taught her to ride side-saddle, the accepted form of riding for young ladies.

Her father believed a girl could do anything a boy could do. And so did Lou. Charles, an amateur naturalist, pointed out grasses, flowers, leaves, and tiny creatures of all kinds as they tramped the Iowa woods.

Lou enjoyed camping out overnight. The sudden hoo-hoo hoo-hoo of an owl did not frighten her. The crickets' song and bullfrog's deep bass lulled her to sleep. She loved waking to morning sunlight with chilly dew frosting the grass.

Lou's mother taught her how to do domestic chores. Sewing was Lou's favorite, although she often felt a tug of war between the domestic skills and the urge to be outside, running and playing.

Florence Henry suffered from bronchial asthma and had to quit teaching school because she was often ill during the damp Iowa winters. In April 1879, after a severe winter, Lou's father decided that a warmer climate would be better for his wife's health. The family left for Corsicana, Texas.

After a three-day train ride, the Henrys arrived at their new home at midnight. The next morning, Lou discovered men sitting on the gallery in shirt-sleeves and roses blooming in the yard.

Lou enjoyed her stay in Texas. She loved the fireplaces with great outside chimneys and the veranda where she could walk all around the house without stepping on the ground.

When the family moved back to Iowa, her parents shared the news that she was going to be a big sister. During her mother's pregnancy, Lou stayed by her mother's side, talking about the baby and sewing tiny clothes. Finally, on June 30, 1882, baby sister Jean was born.

At elementary school, Lou became editor of the school newspaper. She named it the *Boomerang* because she liked the sound of the word.

Charles Henry believed a girl could do anything that a boy could do.

From November on in Iowa it was winter and that meant winter sports: ice skating (her favorite), sledding, tobogganing, building snow forts and snowmen. Waterloo opened an indoor rollerskating rink, and Lou went often. She was agile and athletic and soon became an expert skater. Once she raced twice around the big skating rink in 38 seconds and blew out 19 candles placed as markers along the race course, triumphing over 100 competitors. She won a silk umbrella and was declared rink champion.

Though Iowa held fun activities for Lou, her mother continued to suffer. In 1887, the Henry family left Iowa for good. Lou felt sad leaving her grandparents and her friends behind.

The family traveled to Clearwater, Kansas, where Charles opened a bank with two partners. Because they arrived in spring when the school year was almost over, Lou didn't enter school. She helped her mother with baby Jean and played with her favorite companion, Logan, a big, curly-haired, black bird dog. From a neighbor, Lou learned to paint the beautiful yellow Kansas sunflowers she saw waving over the big land.

But the stay in Kansas was short. The country wasn't developed enough for the bank that Charles had envisioned. He traveled to California and decided the family should move there. The Henrys left for their new home in September 1887.

During the trip west, Lou felt they were pioneers. The Sante Fe and Southern Pacific railroads chugged across the Southwest. She stared out the window as day followed dusty day. At last the train pulled into the Los Angeles station, and Lou stared in awe at the huge metropolis of more than 50,000 inhabitants.

Whittier, California, their destination, was less than a year old.

Florence Weed Hoover holding baby Lou in 1874, the year Lou was born.

Only about a thousand people lived there. Whittier was a Quaker settlement, and the streets and sections of the city were carefully planned. Charles opened his bank in the business section, and the Henry family moved into an apartment over the bank.

In those days, to be a banker meant to have a big iron safe and a set of ledgerbooks. The most important thing a banker needed was the confidence of the people. Mr. Henry inspired respect, so his business prospered.

Soon the Henrys moved to a country bungalow with a large garden and orchard on Painter Avenue. Lou helped her father plant a eucalyptus tree in the yard. She loved their new home.

At first there was no public school in Whittier. Lou and the other children went to Whittier Academy. The top floor of the long narrow store building that the townspeople had converted into a school was for the upper grades and the lower was for the lower grades. Lou, at thirteen, climbed the tall outside stairway. She studied Latin, algebra, advanced geography, history, and advanced English.

After school, and on Saturdays, Lou often went to her father's bank where he let her add columns of numbers. The bank was dim and cool. She loved the inky smell and the feel of the leather-bound books.

At the first public school, Evergreen, Lou looked forward to recess and playing ball. But the playground was a field of tough, dry barley stubble and whenever a ball was hit the game had to be stopped to find it. Lou rallied her classmates to clear the field, dividing them into work squads. She decreed that those who cleared the most stubble would be the winners, and the losers must feed them.

As the students tore into the job, they discovered spiders. Whole-

Lou dressed for ice skating in Waterloo, Iowa, 1884.

sale desertion almost took place, but Lou shouted, "Never mind the spiders! They won't hurt you. But if you see any of the trap-door kind, call me. I want them for my collection." In two hours, the students cleaned the field in every direction as far as their best pitcher could throw a ball. Though Lou's team won, she treated all the workers.

Lou moved on with her class to the Bailey Street School where she studied hard but still had time for walks and drives, some parties, a few dances. Miss DeWolf taught the students and directed them in a class drama. Lou portrayed Joan of Arc. For her costume, Lou carefully snipped clean tops of cans and sewed them on her sweater to make a coat of mail to wear with heavy leather gauntlets.

The Henrys wanted the best for their daughters and were open to new ideas. Though physical activity was not considered appropriate for young ladies and was disguised under the title of "calisthenics," Mrs. Henry believed in the value of exercise and hired an instructor from Los Angeles to give her daughters private lessons.

The Henry home was full of books and Lou read whenever she found time. She looked forward to the monthly arrival of her favorite magazine, *St. Nicholas*. The best part was the "Letter Box." She decided to write her own letter to the magazine. After she sent it, she waited month after month until she almost gave up hope. Then one winter day when the magazine arrived and she turned to the "Letter Box," there was her letter—every word of it.

Lou's parents taught Christianity by example without laying stress on any particular church. Lou often went to meetings of the Quakers, also known as the Society of Friends. Lou agreed in her heart with their teachings that the truth should always be spoken and life lived simply. Like the Quakers, Lou believed in being tolerant of

Lou, standing to the right gazing into the barrel of her rifle, on a school trip in 1889.

The Bailey Street School Fan Drill team. Lou is in the front row, on the left.

people different from herself. When an Episcopalian church was built in Whittier, the Henry family prayed with both the Quakers and the Episcopalians.

Lou looked forward to the times her father could get away from the bank to take her exploring. Lou and "Papa" hiked, rode horseback, camped, and collected rocks, plants, animals. Often they walked four or five miles a day. With her long hair braided, Lou dressed in a hunting suit with a long skirt. She carried the small 22-caliber rifle her father had given her as they roamed the low Puente hills near Whittier, hunting ground squirrels and gophers.

In the spring of 1890, Lou and her class prepared to graduate from ninth grade, the highest, at Bailey Street School. She wrote in an essay entitled "The Independent Girl," that: "She prefers fighting her own battles in this life, and sallies forth to each encounter with a martial spirit which is quite startling."

Lou showed this independence when she organized a fan-drill team. In Quaker Whittier, where dances were frowned on, a fan-drill team was regarded with skepticism. Lou persisted, and drilled the twelve girls until they knew their evolutions and flourishes of fans perfectly.

Graduation day came. Sixteen-year-old Lou put on her graduation dress with its flowing butterfly sleeves and blue-fringed sash and led her team in a colorful whirl of dresses and fans. The criticism melted as rounds of applause followed their performance.

Chapter Two

Stanford Years

In September 1890, Lou entered State Normal School in Los Angeles. She had grown into a tall, slender, vivacious young woman who was an interesting talker. She dressed for school in a dark blue middy blouse of serge, with four-in-hand tie, hair braided at back and tied with a black ribbon.

One professor came to her name on the class list and asked, "Is this name Lou Henry or Henry Lou?" The class laughed and looked at Lou.

Lou excelled at the school gymnasium where the class learned military tactics, club swinging, wand drills, tumbling exercises, and trapeze work.

Charles Henry received an invitation to open a bank in Monterey, California. Lou's parents and Jean moved there. They wrote daily to her at school.

On March 29, 1891, Lou turned seventeen. "It seems so very, very old," she wrote in her diary. Her parents sent her a gold watch and money to buy a tennis racket.

Then summer came at last and with her father she packed gear in a buckboard and headed out into the mountains on her saddle horse. The Los Angeles Ranges include a few peaks that rise above 10,000 feet and beautiful valleys. "Dark canyons beneath us and the lower peaks with their wide-brimmed sombreros of clouds," Lou wrote in her diary.

Breakfast was fresh game and hardtack. She could hunt and fish all day or lie and watch the dark pines silhouetted against the blue sky. She drew sketches of camp life, and thought maybe she would be an artist.

In the evening the blaze of a campfire gathered the campers around to clean a rifle, mend some tackle, or splice a rod as they told stories. As the chilly night wind blew up, stirring the smoldering coals to glow a while longer, they made plans for the next day. Stars in the narrow sky outlined the dark canyon walls as they bedded down. This was the life Lou loved.

Another school year passed. On Tuesday, March 29, 1892, Lou became, "Eighteen at last, a young lady in truth." She finished her term at the State Normal School at Los Angeles in June and joined her family in Monterey. "Monterey is such a funny old place, all adobes, and crooked streets and funny places. I think I will like it very much," Lou wrote in her dairy.

During the summer, Lou helped her father at the bank. She counted and rolled silver and made collections. One of the bank's customers was a young Spanish priest, Rev. Ramon Mestres. Lou admired his progressive ideas and his spirit as he laid out tennis courts, baseball fields, track and other athletic playgrounds. Often when Lou finished work, she and her girlfriends watched ball games or played a game of tennis with Father Mestres.

In September, Lou transferred to San Jose Normal School. As a prospective future teacher, one of Lou's classes was manual training.

Lou posed for this photo while on a camping trip in 1891.

She learned to use a hammer, plane, rip and crosscut saw, square, rule, and a brace.

At last, graduation was only a month away. Lou appealed to her father for help in finding a job. She wrote to him stating that if no teaching position was open, "I want a position in the bank at $275 a month."

Lou graduated on June 23, 1893, and went home to Monterey. No teaching positions were available. She felt unsettled, not knowing what to do, wanting to be able to support herself. She went to work as a cashier at the Monterey Bank.

She taught briefly in the spring of 1894 to fill in for a teacher who left to be married. Lou had wanted to teach geography, history, and higher arithmetic to the older students, but because of her inexperience the school board assigned her to the third grade. She found herself with twenty small children who she felt should be outside playing.

Lou attended a lecture on geology for a summer science class presented by Professor John Casper Branner from Stanford University that captured her imagination. She sought out Dr. Branner after the lecture and explained her deep interest in the earth and its structure. Could a woman study geology at Stanford? He assured her she could. Lou applied for admission and was accepted.

By the time Lou arrived at Stanford in 1894, the three-year-old university had 800 students (250 of them women). Lou set a course for a liberal arts education with a major in geology. For her language requirement, she added Latin. "But I don't know what I shall ever do with Latin," she said.

Dr. Branner taught many of the geology courses. One day in the lab his young assistant, Herbert "Bert" Hoover, came in. Dr. Banner introduced him to Lou. Then he asked the tall, sturdy young man his opinion on the rock specimen he and Lou were discussing. Bert lowered his hazel eyes and stuffed his hands into his corduroy trouser pockets.

On a Saturday evening soon after, Professor and Mrs. Branner invited a few students for dinner. Bert and another young man were asked to bring Lou and another young woman. When the foursome arrived at the Branner home in a heavy rainstorm with dripping raincoats, Bert helped the other young woman with her coat. He'd felt a bit intimidated by Lou.

But when it was time for dinner, Mrs. Branner instructed Bert to escort Lou to the table. Dr. Branner worried that Bert would be miserable, but during dinner they were absorbed in one another's conversation.

Lou working in the Stanford chemistry lab, 1895.

Lou brought Bert out of his shyness by sharing her enthusiasm for Dr. Branner's teachings. They talked about geology and family, discovering they had both been born in Iowa in the same year, she in March, Bert in August. They both moved out west about the same age. Bert, too, loved outdoor life. When the evening was over, Bert told his friend, "That Lou Henry is all right." Lou was different from any girl Bert had ever met. She was boyish, independent, and full of enthusiasm.

The geology class consisted of all young men, except for Lou. When the first field trip was scheduled, the male students discussed whether Lou should be allowed to go or not. They decided she could go once and they would evaluate how she did.

When a fence barred their path, Bert offered his hand to Lou in her long skirt. But she measured the fence with a practiced eye, jogged up, and lightly vaulted over. Her small hat bounced on her head. She settled it with a firm hand as she caught Bert's look and smiled her gap-toothed grin. Bert blushed. There was never again a question if Lou could go.

Lou and Bert often hiked ahead of the group. Bert told her how he'd been orphaned as a young boy and had gone to live with his Quaker uncle in Oregon. He told her about his older brother, Theodore—"Tad"—and his sister, Mary—"May."

Lou's vivaciousness brought Bert with his timid social skills into a whirl of campus activities, and by spring he and Lou attended every major social event.

When Bert graduated and went to work for a U.S. Geological Survey field party, he asked Lou if she would write. "Of course I will," she answered.

Lou went home to Monterey, entertaining college friends and looking forward to Bert's letters from the High Sierras. Unlike Lou, who reveled in horseback riding, Bert detested it. "A horse was one of the original mistakes of creation," he wrote.

The next school year, Jean accompanied Lou to San Jose to study music under a special teacher. Lou felt the weight of being a big sister as she struggled to oversee Jean's music education and to balance their financial obligations.

Meanwhile, Bert was trying to find a more permanent engineering job. When Lou was in her junior year at Stanford, an English firm—Bewick, Moreing and Company—hired Bert to explore mines in West Australia. Before he left, he visited Lou and had dinner with her family. He told her what an excellent position his new job was and that it had a future. Would she wait for him? "Yes," Lou said.

Herbert Hoover as a young mining engineer in West Australia.

Lou and Bert with her parents and sister Jean on the Hoovers' wedding day,
February 10, 1899.

Throughout the next school year, Lou received letters from Bert.
He told her about living conditions in West Australia where "my cook
made a bucket of cocoa and left it setting by the fire to go to the tent.
When he returned not three minutes later, he had to fish 391 flies out
of it."

On May 25, 1898, Lou received her A.B. (Artium Baccalaureus:
Bachelor of Arts) in geology from Stanford. She was the first woman
in the United States to receive a degree in geology.

But when she returned to Monterey to start applying for jobs, she
found out no one wanted to hire a female geologist. Lou launched
into volunteer work and, with her mother, helped found the Monterey-
Pacific Grove Chapter of the American Red Cross.

Then a long telegram arrived from Bert. He had accepted the

position of mining consultant with the Chinese Bureau of Mines. The environment in China would be more hospitable than the outback of Australia, and the position offered a sizeable increase in salary. Would Lou marry him? "Yes," she answered in a one-word telegram.

When Bert arrived from Australia on one of the last days of January 1899, Lou met him at the train station. They chose February 10 as their wedding date so they could catch the boat that sailed from San Francisco for China on February 11.

The Henrys liked Bert. Charles felt his daughter had found a perfect partner. She would be able to keep up with him physically and with her sharp mind and education she'd be his intellectual partner, too. Over the years she had developed a zest for traveling, so life married to a mining engineer seemed ideal for her. Lou was ready to make a home for Bert wherever they went.

On Friday, February 10, Father Ramon Mestres came to the Henry home at noon. Mary and Theodore Hoover and the Henrys gathered in the living room around the couple. Lou and Bert both wore traveling suits, Bert with a high white collar, his straight hair carefully parted in the middle, and Lou with her double-breasted suit jacket open over a beautiful blouse. The wedding service was an adaption of the Catholic service. After a wedding lunch, the newlyweds left for San Francisco.

Chapter Three

Righteous Harmonious Fists

The day after Lou and Bert's wedding was perfect. San Francisco Bay sparkled as the couple boarded the *S.S. Coptic*. For the month it took the steamship to cross the Pacific, Lou and Bert explored the ship, read—they'd bought all the books on China they could find—and made new friends. The talk on board ship was of the Boer War just starting in South Africa.

The *S.S. Coptic* reached China and anchored in the mouth of the *Ch'ang Chiang*, or "long river," known as the Yangtze. Lou and Bert waited in Shanghai until the harbor at Tientsin was free of ice. They explored the city. Gilt and color decorated the shops, but the city was crowded, noisy, and dirty. Soon they traveled north along China's coast to Tientsin.

Tientsin was on the Peiho River. The river was navigable by ocean steamers to the foreign settlement, called the "Concession." This narrow strip of land, eight to ten blocks on three parallel streets, was divided into sections governed by Britain, France, Russia, Japan, and the United States. This was where Lou and Bert would live. The Chinese city itself lay about two miles away, with a maze of Chinese houses in between. Tientsin was about sixty miles southeast of Peking (Beijing), the capital of China.

In the evening they walked through the lantern-lighted streets, smelling the strange incense that floated in the air, listening to the crash and wail of unfamiliar music. An ocean separated Lou from family and all she had ever known, yet she knew this was where she wanted to be.

Within two weeks, Bert began his travels to different mines. Lou was left to care for herself. She read books and studied the reports Bert sent. She mapped the geology of the regions where Bert would be. When Bert returned from his trips, they examined ore. Lou began collecting geological specimens and sending them back to Dr. Branner for the geology department at Stanford.

Lou began taking Chinese lessons. One of her first questions when she got off the boat had been, "Where can I find a teacher of Chinese?" Chuan Yuen-tung became her teacher. Hoo Loo was Lou's Chinese name; Hoo Yah, Bert's.

The Hoovers met neighbors and made friends in the Concession. When Bert was away, Lou wrote to him, sometimes in Chinese. Bert never became a fluent Chinese speaker, but he understood much that was said to him. Later in life, when Lou wanted to say something privately to him in a crowd, she spoke in Chinese.

Occasionally, Lou accompanied Bert on his trips. They traveled by canal boat, carts, mule, and horseback. Armed guards rode ahead to ward off bandits. Once they traveled as far as Lanchou at the Great Wall. Lou sketched the country, the mountains, the rivers, and the people as they went. When they arrived at their destinations, they found people waving banners and shouting welcomes.

They often stayed in inns where Lou's bed was a woven grass mattress and wadded quilt atop a *kang* (the wide brick shoulder of the fireplace). The *kang* stayed warm all night from a tiny charcoal blaze in the fireplace, but it was still a very hard bed.

Lou learned to "type-write" and began writing anecdotes about their life in China. People asked her what magazine she wrote for. Lou just laughed and kept on writing.

By November, ice formed in the harbor, cutting off their link with family. In North China, winter was very long and cold—but it hardly compared to Iowa.

Although Lou loved China, trouble was brewing. The young emperor of China had brought foreigners in to develop mines, build railways, and improve harbors. But some Chinese feared the foreigners would bring foreign rule and customs. The emperor was seized and held under house arrest. His formidable royal aunt, the Empress Dowager, took control of the government.

In the middle of this unrest, in the spring of 1900, a group that called itself *I-ho-ch'uan,* or "Righteous Harmonious Fists," (called the Boxers in English), vowed to rid northern China of all "foreign devils" and any Chinese associated with the foreigners. In one of its first strikes eighty Christian Chinese at Kao Li, a village about a hundred miles from Tientsin, were massacred.

After hearing the news of Kao Li, Bert ordered his staff to go home to the United States. He felt he should remain in China. He begged Lou to leave with the many women and children departing on American and British warships. She refused. Whatever happened, she wanted to be with Bert.

The people in the Concession waited. The Boxers were rumored to be only ten miles away. It was said that on the Chinese Dragon Festival, June 1, the Boxers planned to massacre the foreigners living in the Concession.

The Hoovers' home in Tienstin.

June 1 came and passed quietly. Then on June 5 no train arrived from Peking. Tientsin lost telegraph contact with Peking on June 10. On Saturday, June 16, the Boxers ringed Tientsin and began burning houses and shops between the Concession and the city. That night a great glare of fire filled the midnight sky. In the morning, smoke and blackened, broken walls stood where sun-dried brick houses had been. From nearby warehouses, Bert and his staff dragged sacks of rice, sugar, and peanuts to build defenses along the cross streets and exposed sides of the Concession.

Nearly 1,750 Russian soldiers who hadn't been able to break through to Peking joined the Concession defense. In all, there were 2,566 soldiers, sailors and marines in the Concession, facing 5,000 Chinese regular troops and 25,000 fanatic Boxers.

Lou tried not to think of the possibilities. One man kept asking Bert if he intended to shoot his wife when the Boxers closed in. At last, the Boxers charged, dancing, waving their guns, giving out fiendish howls. Bullets whizzed like torrents of hornets. Shells fell everywhere. The defenders repelled attack after attack.

Many residents took refuge in the town hall toward the center of the Concession. The Hoovers moved to the Drew home, situated in a more central location. Lou bundled food and bedding on her bicycle and rode to the house, where about thirty people set up housekeeping. Lou soon found herself in charge. The food situation was serious, so she organized the people. She rationed food, planned meals, set people to work.

All of the Chinese butchers and bakers had run away, but rice and sugar were abundant—all the defenders had to do was tap the barricades. One of Bert's young engineers rounded up eleven cows and four calves wandering on the plain.

A young English boy took charge of the herd. He had no idea how to change a living cow into meat, so when they needed to butcher a cow, he chopped the cow up with an axe, hide and all. Finally, a British marine was found who knew how to butcher. Chickens ran loose and so they, too, became part of the food supply, along with horse meat. Lou was said to cook horse meat better than anyone else.

The clubhouse became the nursing center. Basic care was given by the one Army doctor, the Concession physician, and one professional nurse. They had no equipment. Stretchers of wounded and dead were brought in every night, until at the end of seven days one soldier in five lay dead or wounded. All of the clubhouse floors were covered with wounded.

Lou inspecting a cannon used to defend Tientsin during the Boxer Rebellion.

Lou rode her bicycle through the Concession, gathering sheets for bandages. She stayed close to the walls of buildings to avoid stray bullets, but a bullet punctured her front tire. She carried a Mauser .38 caliber pistol, but never had to use it. As captain of the guard for her compound, Lou chose men for night watch and took hot tea to the defenders at the barricades.

As the siege wore on, Lou and Bert returned to their own home. One evening, after a long day at the hospital, Lou sat relaxing. With a roar, a shell tore through a back window, exploded and blew out the front door. Lou calmly stood up and said, "That was three (shells) in a row. Let's go have tea now."

By June 19, ammunition was running low. No word came from the outside world. Those in charge wondered if they should try to make a break for Taku. Maybe no one knew how desperate their situation was.

Rumors often flew that help was coming, but the days dragged on. Hearing once more that relief was just across the river, Lou and Bert climbed to the top of the barricade. They saw soliders marching. Welsh Fusileers came first. Then Americans marched into the Concession playing "There'll Be a Hot Time in the Old Town Tonight." The defenders cheered the 700 reinforcements. More allied reinforcements arrived, and they drove the Chinese back. On July 14, the siege ended.

Newspaper correspondents flooded in. Lou said anyone who helped forage for food could stay at their house. Soon the house was crowded. News and letters began to arrive from the outside world. In one newspaper, Lou found her obituary. It was three columns long. "I'll never be this famous again," she said, laughing. She immediately wired their families, telling them of their safety.

When the Boxer Rebellion ended, anarchy reigned across North China. Bert's job was in jeopardy. In August, the Hoovers left China. In spite of the Boxer Rebellion, Lou had come to love China and its people. She wrote a friend, saying that it had been a grand adventure.

Chapter Four

London Years

On board the ship to London, Lou spent much of her time writing about their experiences in China. She hoped to publish a book. When they arrived in London, Lou awoke on Monday, October 1, 1900, to look across the street at Westminster Abbey and the Houses of Parliament. She visited Bert at Bewick, Moreing and Company, and explored along the Thames, Regent Street, Piccadilly and Pall Mall.

Bert was soon asked to return to China to oversee the business, so Lou and Bert headed across the Atlantic. They stopped in New York City, where they gave an interview about the Boxer Rebellion, and then crossed the United States to California.

Lou had been gone for two years. Her parents were happy to have them home and could hardly bear the thought of Lou leaving for China again. Bert thought it might be safer if she stayed in Japan and perhaps Jean could accompany her. So Lou and Jean lived in Yokohama, Japan, while Bert went on to China. Their house had sliding panel doors, paper windows, and straw mats on the floor. They dressed in silk Japanese kimonos.

In the spring, they joined Bert in Tientsin and then sailed to California where Lou and Bert gave Lou's father money to buy land for them so they would have a "mooring" on American soil.

Bert soon became a junior partner in Bewick, Moreing and Company, and he and Lou moved to Australia. Their first station was Kalgoorlie, where they lived in a company house built in the American style.

While Bert worked, Lou investigated and analyzed mines. On horseback, by buggy, and camel, Lou traveled with Bert in the Outback. They traveled 3,500 miles in two-and-a-half months.

When they returned to London, Lou rented a flat for them at Hyde Park Gate. It would be their home for five years. They bought their first automobile, a French Panhard. Lou discovered that she loved to drive, and in one year, 1902, she traveled 2,000 miles through England and Wales, enjoying the countryside.

The Hoovers were becoming rich. In December 1902, Bert sold 15,000 shares of the Chinese Engineering and Mining Company for $75,000. This was a great amount of money for a man who had only had forty dollars in his pocket when he graduated from college. But Lou and Bert agreed that money was not their primary goal in life. Lou wrote to her father that she wished him to use her money to establish an "educational fund and loan it out to people who needed just a little more to finish their education."

Then Bert discovered that the company's chief accountant had used company funds to speculate in the stock market—and lost. He had "borrowed" over a million dollars. Although the company was not legally liable for the accountant's actions, Bert said they would make good on all the losses. Bert shouldered twenty per cent of the loss. It took him until 1907 to pay off the debt.

But the good news was that Bert would be staying in London to deal with the company's financial problems. This made Lou happy because she was expecting their first baby in mid-summer.

Lou and her sister, Jean, often wore Japanese dress during their stay in Yokohama.

Herbert Clark Hoover, Jr. was born on August 4, 1903. He was a fine, healthy son. They planned to leave for Australia in the fall, so Lou prepared to take the newborn around the world.

Special care was given to protect baby Herbert in the Outback. A small folding rubber bathtub that served as a mattress fit inside his large two-handled basket. Home would be wherever they were. The family journeyed on passenger liners, tramp steamers, tugs, railways, motorcar, buggy, horse, and camel. They mingled with public officials and private friends, encountered good people and bad, snobs and crooks, strange people and customs. They ate good food and bad, slept on good beds and bricks, suffered through bugs, dust, sand. Wherever she went, Lou lugged "Mrs. Corona," her heavy black typewriter. She continued to collect rock specimens to send back to Dr. Branner. Eventually, Stanford had one of the most complete

This photo of Lou holding Herbert Hoover, Jr. was taken in Australia in 1903.

geology collections in the world—thanks to Lou.

Back home in London, Lou was delighted when Bert's brother, Theodore, also joined Bewick, Moreing and Company, moving his family to London. It was good to have family near. They visited the London Zoological Gardens and had family dinners and picnics.

Lou found a rambling eight-room house on Camden Hill to lease. The "Red House" had steam heating and large, comfortable bathrooms (which were very uncommon at the time). Outside, a garden and fish pond won Lou's heart. With its high brick wall surrounding the large yard, the "Red House" felt like a country home.

When Bert had to return to Australia, Lou remained at home. She was pregnant. Bert arrived home the day before their second son, Allan Henry Hoover, was born on July 16, 1907. Lou prepared to take the boys on another world trip. This time to Burma.

In Mandalay, Lou found the living conditions very primitive. Frail bamboo houses lined the banks of the Irrawaddy River. Even brick houses had bamboo frames. Pipelines were of split bamboo. At least their cottage was screened and drained.

It was a battle to provide a safe home for the family. Bloodsucking leeches preyed on humans; insects were a serious health hazard, especially to the baby. Small black flies injected an itchy poison. Night-feeding buffalo flies swarmed through the meshes of mosquito nets. Malaria-carrying mosquitoes attacked constantly. In spite of Lou's best efforts, the entire family came down with malaria.

But Lou fell in love with the Burmese people. She helped her husband solve housing and sanitation problems for some families.

Lou enjoyed shopping at the Zegyo. It was a covered bazaar (much like a mall) and one of the finest in the world. Silks, jewels, carved

Lou with a Burmese friend during her 1907 visit to one of her favorite countries.

images in marble and soapstone lined the walkway. After five months Lou and the boys returned to London.

When they were home in London, the Hoovers traveled the English countryside on weekends and holidays. They showed the children the white cliffs of Dover, Stonehenge, the cathedral at Salisbury, the regattas at Henley. Often they stopped so the children—and Bert—could take off their shoes and socks to wade barefoot in streams. They rented summer homes on the Dorset coast and, once, in Shakespeare's town, Stratford-on-Avon.

Every Sunday night the Hoovers gave a dinner in the "Red House." Lou enjoyed entertaining friends and colleagues from America, business associates, mining engineers, foreign dignitaries. Sometimes when the guests arrived, Lou would tell them they could find Bert in the garden. There he would be with Herbert and Allan, splashing around, wading in the fountain's pool or panning for the crushed gold ore Bert had put in the pool for the boys to find.

At dinners, though, Lou kept the conversation going because Bert's shyness caused him to eat silently. Even at family dinners he didn't talk. The Hoover cousins plotted to break that silence, gleefully making a covert game out of who could make him say something. The winner was the one who got him to speak—even "Pass the salt" counted.

But Lou was charming and exuberant and always a good listener. She made everyone feel at home. Lasting friendships grew. Edgar Rickards and his wife, Abby (nicknamed "Abby-his-wife" in true British style), came to live in London in 1909 and soon became lifelong friends of the Hoovers.

Lou filled their home's library with more than 2,500 books. Rows of weighty books on economics, history, sociology, government,

Lou Hoover as she looked during the London years.

geology, mining, metallurgy sat on shelves along with volumes of Sherlock Holmes and other fiction. She continued to write and, in 1909, published an article, "The Late Dowager Empress."

While doing research at the British Museum Library, Lou found a copy of a 16th century book on mining technology, *De Re Metallica*. She recognized it from one of Dr. Branner's classes. It was written in Latin. The book was like the Bible of mining and had been published in 1556 but never accurately translated because readers couldn't understand it. The author, Georgius Agricola, had made up words to explain mining processes and minerals for which there were no Latin words.

She checked out the book and took it home to ask Bert if he would be interested in translating it into English with her. He agreed. She thought the translation would take about a year. They worked on it for the next five years. Lou brushed up on the Latin she had thought she would never use, and Bert performed experiments to try to understand what Agricola was describing. Night after night they worked in their oak-paneled library. When they traveled, the manuscript went with them so they could work on it in their spare time.

When the translation was complete, Lou said it was too bad the California gold rush miners hadn't been able to read the book. They wouldn't have had to re-invent the sluice box, the stamp mill, the hydraulic treatment of ores, amalgamation, because it was all in the book written nearly 400 years before. Lou oversaw the publication. It was dedicated to Dr. Branner.

In 1912, Lou published an article on John Milne, a British seismologist. She also helped Bert research and write a series of lectures he gave at Stanford and Columbia and later published as a book entitled *The Principles of Mining*. She insisted the book include

Lou, Allan, and Herbert, Jr. visiting her parents in 1910.

a chapter on ethics in the mining engineering profession.

On March 9, 1914, the Mining & Metallurgical Society of America presented Lou and Bert with its first gold medal for "Distinguished contributions to the literature of mining." Lou and Bert's scholarly translation of the ancient *De Re Metallica* made it accessible to the modern world. Lou told the diners in her acceptance speech that what had helped her most with the book was "perseverance."

Whenever possible, Lou took her boys to California to visit Grandpa and Grandma Henry and their cousins. The boys loved the California hills just as their mother had.

Lou and Bert decided their sons should have an American education. Lou rented a cottage on the Stanford campus, and Herbert and Allan attended the Campus School. Lou divided her time between California and London.

In London, she and Bert enjoyed Shakespearean plays, Gilbert and Sullivan light operas, and vaudeville. Lou managed their large household staff at the "Red House" and continued to entertain lavishly. She joined the Lyceum League to help promote lectures, concerts, and debates. She became a member of the Society of American Women (the American Women's Club after 1916). The club was active in literary, artistic, scientific, and philanthropic pursuits. Lou remembered that the club had provided a hospital ship to the Allied Forces during the Boxer Rebellion. Lou became chair of the club's education and philanthropic committee and administered a scholarship fund for needy students, supplied Easter dinner to the poor in East London, helped subsidize the Browning Settlement for the homeless, and raised money to buy toys for needy children. Eventually, she became first vice president.

In the spring of 1913, Lou took the boys to visit Bert where he was working in Kyshtim, Russia. The Kyshtim mine was on an old estate that belonged to the ruling Romanov family.

After Christmas, and two months of family time in California, Lou received a cable in May 1914 from the Society of American Women in London. She was now president. When school was out, she and the boys returned to London, sailing aboard the *Lusitania*. Lou had turned forty in March.

In Europe there were threats of war. Age-old hates and rivalries stewed, particularly in the Balkan Peninsula. In July, Austria-Hungary declared war on Serbia, and in August, Great Britain and Germany went to war. World War I had begun.

Chapter Five

The Great War

Lou booked passage on the *Lusitania* so she and the boys could return to California after Bert's birthday. But passage on all ships was canceled when World War I began in late July of 1914, the height of the tourist season. The Americans traveling in Europe poured into London, hoping for safe passage home, only to discover ships not sailing, hotels full, paper money worthless, and even their letters of credit from banks at home not accepted. They flocked to the American Embassy and pounded on the consul's counter.

The American consul called Bert. Did he have any money? Bert took what he had on hand and Lou gave him her household money to loan to the stranded Americans. The Savoy Hotel was letting Americans stay there on credit, but it was filling fast. At the Savoy, Lou saw distraught women, traveling alone or with children, unable to do anything.

Lou called a meeting of the Society of American Women and organized assistance. They set up quarters in the Grand Ballroom of the Savoy and dispensed money and reassurance. Before they were done, they had aided 120,000 Americans.

As wounded soldiers and sailors began arriving, Lou organized the American Women's War Relief Committee. They established the American Women's Hospital.

But Lou felt her sons should be in America. She booked passage on the *Lusitania* and they sailed October 3. From California she cabled Bert: "Herbert, Allan, Mummy, white rabbits, baby chickens, toads, frogs, lizards, salamanders, silk worms, and horned toad all well and send love."

Across the world people were not "all well." Belgium had been invaded and was under German rule, so Britain blockaded its ports. No food could come in. Famine loomed. There wasn't enough food to keep people alive for three weeks. Loaves of bread made with straw, clay, sawdust, and even manure were eaten to fill hollow stomachs.

The neutral nations planned a large-scale relief effort and asked Bert to lead it. He cabled Lou to ask her advice. She thought he should say "yes." His acceptance of the position began Bert's public career.

Food didn't come free. Lou told her sister, Jean, "I'm really scared to death to speak publicly," but she spoke anyway to San Francisco businessmen and trustees of Stanford to seek assistance. She raised $100,000 and secured a shipload of food. She persuaded the Rockefeller Foundation to provide free shipping of food and clothing to Belgium. Aid continued to come in from Stanford's students in the form of monthly pledges.

By October the Central Powers—Germany, Austria-Hungary, and the Ottoman Empire—were at war with the Allies—Great Britain, Belgium, France, Russia, and Serbia. Other countries joined in, but the United States remained neutral. After a special Thanksgiving Day spent with her sons, Lou prepared to return to London.

Realizing she was to journey through submarine-infested waters and might never see her sons again, she appointed a friend, Jackson E. Reynolds, to supervise their education. In a letter she instructed him to be sure her sons had an American education and not let them set a monetary value on life.

The steely gray, wintery Atlantic Ocean dotted with warring ships rolled as Lou's ship made its way across. It was a nerve wracking journey, but she arrived safely in London. Lou and Bert traveled to Belgium and saw starving people, burned-out buildings with empty window spaces, and heard hobnailed German boots echoing on brick streets. People stood in line in cold rain, clutching their ration cards, grasping their empty bowls, waiting for food. Lou saw the "baby-kitchens," where mothers received milk for their babies or rich soups for "babies under three and over seventy-five." All classes of people came to the canteens.

After a sad Christmas Eve dinner spent at the American Legation in Brussels, Lou returned to London with a sore heart. She missed her sons terribly, but she threw herself tirelessly into the war effort.

Lou wrote articles for American newspapers, describing what she had seen and what was needed. In the United States, newspapers collected funds, pastors preached on Belgium's need, Granges contributed food, clubs donated funds for barrels of flour. "Belgian" days and "Dollar-a-Month" pledges raised funds. "Lunch boxes" to support infants and families could even be bought in restaurants.

Lou stood with other women at railway stations to hand out sandwiches and coffee to servicemen. In Belgium, 50,000 women and girls desperately needed work to provide food for their families. Lou began a campaign to sell Belgian lace. The Commission for

Relief provided thread and bought the lace and the Germans permitted the lace to be exported as long as no political motifs were embroidered on it.

In April 1915, Lou planned to return to America for a money-raising tour for war relief but missed booking passage on the *Lusitania*. On May 7 a German submarine sank the *Lusitania*. Over a thousand people died, including 128 Americans. Lou sailed safely across the Atlantic on another ship.

Bringing her strength and enthusiasm for the cause with her, Lou began her speaking tour in New York City. When she finished, she went home to her sons in California. They spent a summer with grandparents and cousins and went on camping trips.

In August, Bert cabled that he thought it was safe for the family to return to London. Upon their arrival, Lou enrolled the boys in a British school near the "Red House."

But beginning in late 1915 the Germans sent dirigibles and airplanes to bomb London. One night in 1916 a bomb hit dangerously near. Lou ran to the boys' room, but they were not in their beds. She and Bert ran frantically through the house and yard, looking for their sons. Then Lou remembered the trap door from the attic to the roof. She raced upstairs and onto the roof. There the boys sat, watching the searchlights and fighting planes. They saw a Zeppelin brought down in flames north of London.

By the end of 1916, with Zeppelins in the air, Lou and Bert decided London was not the place to bring up their sons. Lou prepared to leave the "Red House," knowing in her heart she would never see it again.

In January 1917, Lou and the boys sailed on one ship and Bert on another for fear the whole family would be lost at sea if a submarine

The Hoovers boarding a ship for the trip to the United States, January 1917.

sank them. They all arrived in New York harbor safely. Lou and her sons settled down in California. Bert soon returned to London.

On April 16, 1917, the United States entered the war against Germany. President Woodrow Wilson asked Bert to head the United States Food Administration.

In California, Lou received the news of Bert's appointment with mixed feelings. Though she was proud of President Wilson's confidence in her husband, she had hoped the family could settle down in California at last.

Instead, the family moved to Washington, D.C., and rented a house that soon overflowed with Food Administration staff. The house, built for eight people, now held some forty men. Lou joined in the effort to devise ways to encourage Americans to conserve food and fuel. "Food Will Win the War," became the rallying cry. The rules were simple: Go back to simple food, simple clothes, simple pleasures. Pray hard, work hard, sleep hard and play hard.

Lou found a bigger house on Massachusetts Avenue where they could plant a large garden in the spring.

The family used no butter or lard, but substituted corn or vegetable oil. Potato breads and biscuits took the place of wheat bread. They ate cornbread every morning. Hominy, oatmeal, and other cereals filled the grain dietary requirement. Fish and game replaced pork and beef. Honey and molasses took the place of sugar. Puddings replaced cakes and pastries. When the boys had a Halloween party, Lou served popcorn rather than cookies.

Americans cooperated and saving food became a way of life. Housewives adopted Lou's recipes for rye and soya bean pie crusts. Restaurants eliminated wheat products. Wheatless and meatless days became standard. Everyone tried to "Hooverize," to cut down on wheat, meat, and sugar, and carefully clean one's plate. Even Eleanor Roosevelt, wife of the young assistant secretary of the Navy, said her family "Hooverized."

Wartime in the capital brought large numbers of young women there to work. They needed decent living quarters and wholesome meals at a reasonable cost. Lou and her friend Abby organized a Food Administration Club to help. She chaired the housing sub-committee that leased, remodeled, and furnished a home for several girls, providing the start-up money out of her own funds. Eventually, she managed to establish three homes, loaning or giving much of the money to run them.

Working with young women helped Lou become aware of the war work being done by the Girl Scouts of America: selling bonds, knitting sweaters and socks for soldiers, taking care of children so mothers could work in war industries. Juliette Gordon Low invited Lou to join in the work. At the time the Girl Scout organization was controversial because it encouraged girls to be independent. Active girls tramping in the woods and camping were frowned upon by society.

But Lou studied the organization and felt it was the best "character building" agency available for girls. She said: "Girl Scouting is so broad in its application, so deep in its significance, so altogether marvelous in its possibilities, that it seems to me the most worthwhile thing on which I can spend that part of my time which is not demanded by my individual responsibility to my family, my friends, my community, and my nation."

Lou charged into Girl Scouting. "I was a Scout years ago, before the movement ever started, when my father took me fishing, camping, and hunting. Then I was sorry that more girls could not have what I had. When I learned of the movement, I thought, here is what I always wanted other girls to have."

That August, Belgium recognized Lou and Bert for all of the help they had given them. A letter came to Lou, stating: "I am happy to announce, my dear Mrs. Hoover, that H.M. Queen Elizabeth, Queen of the Belgians, has so fittingly bestowed on you the Medal of Queen Elizabeth in appreciation of your splendid and untiring contribution toward the relief of Belgium."

1918 brought another devastating blow—a worldwide influenza epidemic. By the fall 300,000 people had already died in the United States and 800,000 in Europe—more people than were killed in the war. When many of the young wartime working women became ill, they were a long way from home. Lou organized nursing care in the Food Administration Club dormitories. She saw that their families were informed of their illness, and sometimes of a young woman's death. None of the Hoovers caught the disease and the epidemic gradually passed.

The German government signed an armistice on November 11, 1918, ending the war. The Food Administration was transformed into an agency for reconstruction and relief. Lou and the boys went to the dock in New York to see their daddy off to Europe again. Then they went home to California, and Lou began making architectural sketches of the dream home she planned to build on land they had leased on the Stanford campus.

Lou missed Bert and was disappointed that she couldn't be with him to help. But she believed that with loyalty and love, people could work together even when apart. With the boys in school, Lou began traveling and organizing banquets to raise money for the starving people of Europe. Plain food was served in tin utensils at these banquets, with an empty high chair for the "Invisible Guest," a hungry child. At one banquet in New York City, a thousand guests paid $1,000 a plate to attend. A special collection that night brought in another million, and John D. Rockefeller gave a third million.

That fall, after Lou and Allan had been to Paris to visit Bert, Lou received a telegram: "By royal Decree Mrs. Hoover just been appointed Chevalier Order Leopold I." King Albert, Queen Elizabeth, and Crown Prince Leopold III came to the United States to confer the Cross of Chevalier, Order of Leopold, on Lou Hoover, in recognition of her relief work on behalf of Belgium.

Lou said, "I have done nothing extraordinary . . . and have tried to be of whatever assistance I could." She told King Albert that what she treasured most were the thousands of thank-you letters from the children of Belgium.

Chapter Six

Girl Scouts

When Bert returned home from Europe, the couple hoped for time to organize the information on the Great War that he had collected in Europe. They planned to give it to Stanford University because they thought that if the causes of war were analyzed countries would know how to build peace.

But instead of a quiet time, the entire country seemed to have an after-war headache. Inflation, strikes, race riots, and Red (communist) scares threw the country into turmoil. Bert was called upon to help ease the national anxiety. Once more he boarded a Pullman and traveled the country giving speeches.

Lou threw herself into building their new home on San Juan Hill on the Stanford campus. She told Allan that she wanted the house to be "elastic," with no particular historical style. Instead, she designed a house that had a Pueblo look but also an Algerian motif, with various elevations. Every flat roof, accessible by outer stairways, and every terrace became a room for out-of-door living. Lou still loved fireplaces, so one was built in every main room and one outdoors for cook-outs. Allan wanted a swimming pool, and Lou saw that a tennis court was built, too.

Because Bert needed to be in New York City, they rented a furnished apartment there, and Lou divided her time between Bert in New York and their sons in California.

Lou had only settled into her dream home when Warren G. Harding was elected president in 1920 and Herbert Hoover was named secretary of commerce. The Hoovers moved back to Washington, where Lou found a spacious, colonial house with 22 rooms on an acre surrounded by great oak trees.

In the fall, Herbert, Jr. returned to California to live with his Uncle Theodore and to graduate from Palo Alto High School. Allan stayed in Washington.

Lou now needed a secretary and eleven servants to help with all her work. Because of Bert's position in the cabinet, the Hoovers often entertained. Lou gave many teas, and almost every evening they had guests for dinner.

Lou, in her black velvet dress, was still the same exuberant person who had helped defend against the Boxers in China. Her handshake was firm and her smile was warm. One time a friend asked Lou how she did all of that entertaining. She replied, "I never entertain. I just ask people to come and see us and we enjoy each other." She helped people in public service in Washington forget how far they were from their own homes and families.

In the summer of 1921, Lou's father cabled her that her mother had died. Lou crossed the continent by train with a heavy heart. Her father and Jean met her when she arrived. She wanted to take her father home with her to live, but he refused.

Back in Washington, Lou embraced the new opportunities for women. She supported programs for children's health and welfare, physical activities, and community service. As always, though, she first attended to her family. But with so many new inventions to make housework easier, she felt women could now have careers after marriage.

The Girl Scout movement became Lou's primary outside interest. In 1921 she became the national vice president of the Girl Scouts, and in January 1922, she was elected national president. She was unanimously re-elected in 1924. By then, the Girl Scouts had grown from about 15,000 to over 110,000.

In 1922 Lou also became leader of her own Girl Scout Troop 8. Twenty girls, fifteen to eighteen years old, were the first Senior Scout Troop, and Lou loved to be with them. She laughed with them and was more than their equal in camp or in the woods. This was her troop until she left Washington.

Lou's philosophy of leadership was to "lead from behind." She suggested, encouraged, and gave example without stating what needed to be done. "We want to accompany rather than lead," she said. She stressed competence as mothers and homemakers along with athletic ability and a love of nature. She said, "It takes just as much courage to stick to the housework until it is done as it does to go out and meet a bear." To Lou, the secret of Girl Scout work was to gain real joy. All depended on attitude: Work considered work became labor; work done with the right attitude became fun.

Lou also felt an important aspect of scouting was recreation. She believed play influenced a person's growth as much as work and studies. "Every young girl should have the opportunity of learning, out-of-doors by first-hand observation, the wonders and loveliness nature has spread so lavishly—and how it grows," she said.

Lou dressed in her Girl Scout uniform, 1925.

Passing on knowledge she had gained from her father and at Stanford, Lou led the girls on long hikes over hills and meadows, pointing out rocks, birds, and trees. She helped the scouts analyze the rocks they found. Secrets of campfire cooking opened up under her direction. The best part was an evening spent around the campfire, telling stories. To Lou, the "outing" was the most important part of Scouting. Lou wrote numerous article for the Girl Scout magazine, *American Girl.*

Lou also turned her attention to other needs. When the National Amateur Athletic Federation (NAAF) was organized in 1922, Lou was invited to be a vice president, the only female officer. She accepted and went to work.

Lou called for the development of a separate division for women because she felt women's standards and purposes were different. Inequities abounded in existing recreation programs. Young men's sports usually had first use of available gyms, the best equipment, the best coaches. Qualified women coaches were scarce. Young women were shut out of many sports entirely. People in the 1920s believed certain physical activities diminished womanliness, so they saw nothing wrong with these inequities. Lou disagreed.

At the time in America, newspaper and radio coverage of athletic events was growing rapidly, promoting sports heroes. Commercial exploitation exploded. The trend became a few "stars" playing and everyone else watching so-called spectator sports.

Educators and physicians were becoming concerned about the growing emphasis on competitive sports for women. They were worried about women who trained under male coaches and competed in the Olympics. The young women's health could be at risk.

Lou and the Girl Scouts working in a war garden in 1918.

The purpose of the NAAF was the promotion of wholesome sports, so Lou convened and chaired the first National Conference on Athletics and Physical Education for Women and Girls. Among the points resolved was the encouragement of participation for all. The value of the game should be participation and education rather than winning. Good sportsmanship and character building should be the goal rather than the making and breaking of records and the winning of championships. "Put fun back into sports," Lou said.

Lou sent the resolutions out to her many friends, to the YMCA and YWCA, to public school physical educators, officials of the American Physical Education Association, National Playground Association, government officials, medical doctors.

Within weeks, dozens of colleges and organizations became members of the NAAF. Gradually, intramural sports and instruction in physical education found a place in schools. Women's organizations developed programs emphasizing active lifestyles. Young people discovered the fun of sports.

Lou also called for research into improving and increasing food supplies, the elimination of waste, the conservation of resources, and the clearing of the air and water.

Lou encouraged women to participate more in politics. She reminded them that their civic responsibility did not end with acquiring the right to vote—it began. "Bad men are elected by good women who stay home from the polls on election day," she said.

Chapter Seven

First Lady

In the summer of 1923, as Lou and Bert accompanied President Harding's tour across the country and to Alaska, the "Teapot Dome" scandal, one of the most destructive episodes in American political history, broke out. Harding's interior secretary was accused of secretly leasing oil fields near Teapot Dome, Wyoming, to an oil company for personal gain. As the scandal grew, it became clear that many members of the Harding Administration were involved in dishonest behavior. Bert was one of the few members of Harding's administration untainted by this and the other scandals that followed.

The strain of the controversy proved to be too much for the president. On the return trip from Alaska, President Harding fell ill and died in San Francisco.

Vice President Calvin Coolidge became president. His wife Grace, a talkative, fun-loving person, in contrast to "Silent Cal," was a close friend of Lou's.

President Coolidge kept Bert as his secretary of commerce. After the funeral and the transition to a new administration, Lou left the hot Washington summer for California. With her sons, niece and nephew, and her father, she vacationed. They pitched camp near a mass of hissing, steaming hot springs in Sonoma County where Lou

Lou and Bert with Florence Harding during the ill-fated Alaska trip.

reminded everyone "Don't put soap in the geysers." They went on
to Siskiyou County for two weeks of hunting and fishing. Then Lou
returned to the busy Washington whirl.

In the spring of 1924 Lou, chairman of the Washington chapter
of the Women's National Committee for Law Enforcement, joined
a nationwide campaign to enforce laws, particularly prohibition. The
Eighteenth Amendment of the Constitution prohibited the manufac-
ture, sale, or transportation of intoxicating liquors. Yet normally-law-
abiding citizens ignored the law and bought "bootleg" alcohol. Even
government officials, including President Harding when he was
alive, broke the law.

Bert supported prohibition until it was repealed, but he considered
himself a wine connoisseur, and had kept a well-stocked wine cellar.
Lou, determined to set an example by obeying the law, emptied out

Florence and President Harding join Lou, Bert and General John Pershing at the opening of the 1922 major league baseball season.

their wine. Bert sighed and told his friends, "I don't have to live with the American people, but I do have to live with Lou."

Other programs called on Lou. She helped raise $100,000 for the Visiting Nurse Society, declaring it the best disease-prevention educational agency in the city. She served on the building committee of the Washington YWCA and made sure a gymnasium and swimming pool were included in the plans. When the Committee of Congressional Women published *The Congressional Cookbook*, Lou not only contributed her own recipes for preparing moose, elk, deer, and bear, she also broadcast a speech about the recipes and the lessons in home economics contained in the cookbook.

With all of her commitments to various causes, though, Lou still believed in saving time for quiet thought. She advocated "an hour alone." This was not for routine rest, but was to be a time to think, to enjoy. "We can control our lives. Like a person riding in a motor car, we can race rapidly through life or else stop along the way and enjoy the scenery." She emphasized the power of personal choice.

The boys were busy, too—Allan in high school and Herbert at Stanford. In June 1924, Herbert's engagement to Margaret Watson was announced. They were both juniors at Stanford. Lou gave an engagement dinner at their home on San Juan Hill, and Bert hurried across the continent to be there.

Then Allan entered Stanford, and Lou found it hard to believe her younger son was in college.

The wedding of Herbert and Margaret—"Peggy"—took place in June 1925. On March 18, 1926, Peggy Ann Hoover was born, Lou and Bert's first grandchild. Lou rushed to Cambridge, Massachusetts, where Herbert, Jr. was taking post-graduate courses, to greet her new granddaughter. It was wonderful to have a little girl in the family. Lou

Lou and Bert with President Coolidge, his wife, Grace, and his son John Coolidge.

stayed for two weeks and then returned to her own busy schedule at her husband's side.

The country was on a great economic boom during Coolidge's presidency. In that year 800,000 new homes were built. New highways crossed the land. Automobile sales exploded. But Bert cautioned the president that the stock market was dangerously inflated. Credit was too easy. Most Americans believed good times had come to stay.

In August 1927, President Coolidge surprised the nation when he announced, "I do not choose to run for president in 1928." Privately, Grace Coolidge reported, "Papa [Coolidge] says there's going to be a depression."

Many people thought Herbert Hoover would make an ideal president, and he had the backing of many loyal friends and high-ranking Republicans. When Bert told Lou he had agreed to have his name placed on the Ohio primary ballot, she welcomed this new opportunity for service though she understood, at least as much as she could at the time, the sacrifice it would be.

Family responsibilities were still first for Lou. On November 5, 1927, Herbert Hoover III was born to Herbert and Margaret.

In June 1928, Allan attended the Republican National Convention in Kansas City as a page. In the big convention hall plastered with posters of his father, he heard his father nominated for president on the first ballot. Bert would officially be notified of his nomination at their legal residence at Palo Alto, so the Hoovers began the train journey across the continent.

On the trip Lou received a telegram from Allan. Her father had taken ill on a hike and was in the hospital. At Omaha, Lou received news that he had died on July 21.

Jean met her at the station in California and together they mourned. But after the funeral, the campaign could not be put off any longer. Bert resigned as secretary of commerce and began his bid for the presidency.

At first, Lou was reluctant to campaign with her husband. She had a new grandson to get acquainted with, as well as her own work. She received an honorary degree of Doctor of Literature from Whittier College, the first woman so honored, for her humanitarian and literary accomplishments.

But in the fall, Lou joined Bert in the campaign. They traveled by rail. She stood on the train's rear platform with him, and even occasionally gave a short speech. She said, "I enjoy campaigning because my husband makes the speeches and I receive the roses."

The Hoover family return to Palo Alto to await election results, November 5, 1928.

For election day, Lou and Bert headed home to California to vote. On election night family, neighbors and friends gathered at their house, crowding around radios, as news began to trickle in. As the results became clearer, Herbert, Jr. and Allan could hardly contain their excitement. The official report boomed from the national radio hookup Herbert, Jr. had set up in the garage. Bert had won! He had carried 40 out of 48 states. He was to be the thirty-first president of the United States.

John Philip Sousa and his band marched up the hill from Stanford and gave a rousing serenade to the president-elect and his family. Bert and Lou, holding excited Peggy Ann, waved to the crowd from their terrace. Herbert and Margaret, holding baby Peter (Herbert III) were there, along with Allan. Students sang the university's alma mater. Telegrams and letters began pouring in. One came from Lou's Chinese teacher, Chuan Yuen-tung.

Newspapers and magazines extolled what a perfect first lady Lou would make. They praised her as an outstanding hostess and noted that she spoke several languages—certainly a plus for someone who would be meeting people from all over the world. One writer said she was about five feet six inches, "but with her erect slenderness appeared taller." Another said she seemed to be the height of whomever she was talking to because her sparkling blue-gray eyes looked so directly. Her step was "light enough not to crack a twig in the woods." Her white hair was softly done, parted in the middle.

Most of all, reporters told the anxious public, she had a "plucky spirit." They also reassured the public that she helped her husband "in every big and small thing."

Heavy storm clouds hovered over Washington D.C. the morning

Bert and Lou on their way to the 1929 Presidential Inauguration.

of March 4, 1929, inauguration day. Lou and the family gathered around Bert in their S Street home. Then the cars arrived and drove them to join President and Mrs. Coolidge. Bert rode to the capitol with Coolidge and Lou rode with Grace. When they left the cars, Lou and Grace became engulfed by the crowd of 100,000 people filing into the grandstands erected outside the East Portico of the Capitol. Rain began to fall. Lou could see the canvas-covered platform ahead, but they couldn't get to it.

When Bert reached his place, he looked around for Lou. Aides spotted the wives trying to make their way and cleared a path for them. Chief Justice William Howard Taft rose with Bert, and Lou watched Bert place his hand on the Bible. "I solemnly swear to faithfully execute the office of the president of the United States and will to the best of my ability preserve, protect, and defend the Constitution," Bert swore. Lou felt certain her husband, the most respected humanitarian of the time, would be the best president ever.

The Hoovers drove to the White House now as the president and first lady. Chief usher "Ike" Hoover (no relation) opened the car door, and Bert, who as president must always go first now, got out. Then Lou, not quite fifty-five years old, tall, statuesque, handsomely dressed in dark, plum-colored velvet, with a velvet hat to match, alighted and ascended the steps to their new home.

The White House is an American shrine, and Lou entered as a mistress fit for the role. From an educational standpoint, no former first lady surpassed her, and in travel and worldly knowledge, her experiences exceeded all. Some first ladies came without ever having set foot in the White House, but Lou had visited often.

Bert and Lou entered the front door and walked into the long, wide corridor on the main floor that ran between the East Room at one end and the State Dining Room at the other. The Hoovers, with their family and friends, were escorted to the second floor's private apartments. There, a buffet luncheon was served and many telegrams delivered.

Lou set about putting her new home in order. The White House comes with its own management, so it is always in running order, but each first lady manages it the way she wants. Although it was a large, beautiful house filled with valuable stores of silver, gold, and China, it is not very convenient. Lou looked at the White House, sized it up, and pronounced it "bleak as a New England barn."

Lou set to work adding their personal belongings brought over from the S Street house, including their grand piano. She covered floors with colorful rugs brought back from South America. She had bookcases built for their many books and placed their objects from all over the world along the tops.

Upstairs, Lou turned the Oval Room into a family parlor where the grandchildren could play and she and Bert could sit by the fire. She transformed the second floor West Hall into an inviting room filled with bookcases, potted palms, wicker furniture, and cages with singing birds. Later she set up a movie projector there so she could show the movies she filmed. As always, Lou fixed up a place with a special box of toys and doll furniture for small visitors to play.

Lou loved her new home and came into the White House graciously and calmly serene. She didn't know that her heart would be broken while she lived there.

Chapter Eight

Great Depression

The Hoovers entered the White House as the richest occupants in many years. Bert served as president without pay. They also spent their own money to make the White House look and run the way they wanted. They paid for all special foods and entertainments above the allotted amount, and for the daily meals of their personal staff.

The staff consisted of about sixty people, with extra part-time help for special events. Lou helped manage all of them. She met with the housekeeper daily to go over menus. New employees always were interviewed by Lou, and once hired, she became very protective of them. One White House butler suffered from tuberculosis, and she made sure he received proper medical care. Another butler who had ulcers and could not afford the cream and milk his doctor prescribed, discovered milk and cream delivered on his doorstep, courtesy of the first lady.

The Hoovers brought their cars with them. Lou loved to drive and wasn't about to stop just because she was first lady. Her Secret Service agent had to race after her in his own car wherever she went.

The first lady had two definite functions to perform: Manage the White House and attend to her official responsibilities. Certain White House traditions had to be observed. Although the Hoovers were not formal people and much preferred casual, comfortable visiting, they respected tradition. Lou performed the traditional official entertainments with grace and good humor: Four evening receptions, four state dinners, four afternoon musicales in the winter; four garden parties in the spring, and the New Year's Day reception open to all.

On January 1, 1930, their first New Year's Day in office, Bert and Lou shook hands with 6,348 people. People expected only a handshake from the president, but almost everyone wanted something more from the first lady—a smile, a few kind words. Lou more than met their expectations.

Under the Hoovers, the entertainments were mammoth. They invited guests for breakfast, lunch, and dinner. Chief Usher Ike said, "They set the best table that was ever set in the White House."

Lou gave many teas, sometimes three in one afternoon. One tea Lou gave, though, caused an uproar. At that time, Washington was a segregated capital. But the Hoovers resisted discrimination. Oscar DePriest, a congressman from Illinois, was the first African-American elected to Congress in thirty years. Lou invited Mrs. DePriest to the traditional tea for congressmen's wives. Tea and cakes were served, with Lou sitting next to Mrs. DePriest. The women visited. Then the tea was over.

A national dispute erupted. Editors of some Southern newspapers accused Lou of "defiling" the White House. The Georgia, Florida, and Texas legislatures passed resolutions reprimanding Lou. The *Mobile Press* said Lou committed an "arrogant insult. That the two races should intermingle at afternoon teas or other functions is inadmissible." But the Topeka *Plain Dealer* praised her: "She put into practice the brotherhood of man." *The Nation* congratulated her "for the human decency of her act."

The ugly controversy deeply hurt Lou. But she stood by her decision and kept her silence. Her friendliness toward the press was never the same after this event. But she remained a warm and gracious, very popular first lady. *Time* magazine featured Lou on the cover of its May 15, 1929, issue and a feature article told the story of her "Open Door" policy.

As first lady, Lou brought performing artists, particularly young American artists, to the White House. She held afternoon musicales, and concerts after state dinners. The Hampton and Tuskegee choirs were the first African-American groups to sing in the White House since 1882. Chief Yowlache of the Yakima performed beautiful Zuni chants. One of Lou's favorite performers was Mildred Dilling, a young harpist from Marion, Indiana.

Lou invited foreign artists, too. One young Russian pianist, Vladimir Horowitz, played his first concert at the White House. He played brilliantly, but he was more concerned because he couldn't speak English very well. Lou told him just to say, "I am delighted," when people greeted him in the receiving line. Horowitz shook his head in agreement and then greeted each passing dignitary with, "I am delightful!"

History was one of Lou's interests, and the historic White House became her research project. She hired Signal Corps photographers at her own expense to take pictures of every piece of furniture. With her secretary's help, she inventoried and catalogued the antiques. The room that had been Abraham Lincoln's office became Bert's study, furnished with Lincoln memorabilia. The Rose Parlor was converted into the Monroe Room. Lou had President James Monroe's desk, where he had written the Monroe Doctrine, reproduced, along with some of his other furniture.

Lou, Bert, and members of the White house staff await their New Year's Day guests, January 1, 1930.

Lou devotedly filled her position as first lady, but the duties often overshadowed the privileges. Her office was a sitting room connected to her bedroom, and piles of papers covered her bed. The White House staff had never seen a first lady work so hard before. They said she worked like a "day laborer." She wanted to make the world a more decent place to live. And she refused to hide Lou Henry Hoover under Mrs. Hoover, wife of the president. "Be yourself," was her motto.

Radio was beginning to play an important role in the lives of Americans. On April 19, 1929, the voice of a first lady was heard over the radio for the first time in history. Lou spoke on the radio at the dedication of Constitution Hall in Washington, the new home of the Daughters of the American Revolution. Major John Goffe, Jr., Lou's ancestor, had been one of those "who assisted in establishing American Independence." Bert, however, didn't care much for speaking on the radio. When an admirer asked if he got a thrill from it, Bert replied, "The same thrill I get when I talk to a doorknob."

Lou took pride in her husband's work as president. She walked with him to his office at the White House executive offices every morning, and they talked about the programs and projects he had in mind. There was so much he could do for good now that he was president.

During his first few months in office, Bert went after gangsters, including Al Capone. He called for increased conservation efforts, commitments to national parks and wildlife refuges, adding about three million acres to the national forest system. The Great Smoky Mountains National Park and the Canyon de Chelly National Monument were among the areas preserved during his administration.

When Bert established bird sanctuaries, Lou's Girl Scouts went to work banding birds. He planned for a new federal Department of

This photo of Lou was used for the May 13, 1929, cover of *Time* magazine.

Education and held a White House Conference on Child Health and Protection. He revived the American Indian economy and began devising an old-age pension plan. The press praised Bert's work, saying, "The White House had become a positive force."

Though Bert had told the American people in his inaugural address that the future of the country was "bright with hope," he was deeply concerned about how people were borrowing money to speculate in the stock market. He called it "crazy and dangerous" and tried to persuade bankers to stop lending money to stock speculators.

Less than eight months after Bert's inauguration, in October 1929, stock market prices plummeted. On one day, October 29, desperate speculators sold more than 16 million shares. This was the beginning of a great economic depression, but few people thought it would last long. The president and business leaders assured the nation that prosperity was "just around the corner."

Bert worked day and night to try to reverse the economic downtrend. The twinkle in his eye turned dull. Even their grandchildren failed to bring out his playfulness. He asked Congress to spend large amounts of money for public works to provide temporary jobs until conditions improved. Public buildings, dams, highways, harbors, and inland waterways were begun. The Bureau of Reclamation started the Boulder Canyon Dam (Hoover Dam) on the Colorado River.

Lou felt Bert needed a break from time to time and that it was her responsibility to see he got it. To Lou, relaxation meant being out of doors, enjoying nature. But where could they go close by?

Lou began roaming the surrounding country to look for camp sites close to Washington. With a Marine Corps detachment riding with her, Lou scoured the Blue Ridge Mountains. Marines watched in

Lou announcing what the Girl Scouts had done to help President Hoover's Emergency Committee, March 24, 1931.

disbelief as she climbed perilous slopes.

At last she found a spot "at the end of nowhere," and Lou purchased the 200-acre plot of land, 109 miles from Washington. There the Mill Prong and Laurel Prong fell over large rocks to form the Rapidan River that had been named by the Virginia settlers in honor of Queen Anne. During the Civil War, General Lee had an observation post there.

Lou drew up the plans. It must have a place, like a Girl Scout mess hall, for eighteen to twenty people to eat. It must have field stone fireplaces. Bert must have a study, and Lou a work room where she could leave her papers scattered about. Their cabin must be near the stream so Bert could hear its murmuring.

Tents served the week-end campers at first, but within a year the large L-shaped "Town Hall" for dining and meeting was built along with Lou and Bert's lodge incorporating a majestic old hemlock. The cabins had deck-like log porches where people could sit out as if they were in the forest. Other cabins were built for family and visitors and quarters for the staff. At first everyone rode in on horseback, but Bert complained of saddle sores, so a road was eventually built. On weekends Lou drove, leading a caravan of cars rapidly up the winding two-lane road into the mountains.

Here Bert could fish. Lou and he had time to walk through the woods, hand in hand. In the evening, they could sit alone in the lodge before the fire in the great stone fireplace, tossing pine cones into the flames, lost in thought or sharing their ideas.

But the economic crises didn't go away. Visitors, including British Prime Minister MacDonald, filled the calendar at Camp Rapidan, and often Bert worked just as hard while he fished or sat on the porches. Weekend guests helped move boulders to create trout

Lou and Bert on a newly built bridge at Camp Rapidan.

pools while the nation's policies were discussed.

One day a boy from nearby Dark Hollow came to camp to give Lou an opossum he'd shot. Lou thanked him and talked to him for awhile, only to discover he didn't go to school. There was no school.

Lou and Bert found that no school had been available to the children of the area for several years. Plans were drawn, and, at their own expense, the Hoovers built a modern schoolhouse and hired a teacher. When the President's School opened in 1930, seventeen pupils, ranging in age from six to seventeen, enrolled.

Not all problems in the country were solved so simply. The stock market crash had affected everyone, not just bankers and rich people, and the country sank steadily into the worst depression in history. By the end of 1930, more than six million Americans were out of work; by 1931, the number rose to twelve million. Consumer goods flooded the market but no one could buy. Banks went broke, factories closed, corner stores were gobbled up by chains. Empty trains ran between silent cities where no smoke came from factory smokestacks. The "American Dream" of prosperity had turned into a cruel joke.

Millions of people lost everything. Men sold apples on street corners, trying to earn a few dollars to feed their families. Soup kitchens and bread lines stretched longer and longer. Churches and other voluntary organizations found it increasingly difficult to raise enough money to feed the hungry.

Those who lost their homes gave their children away to those who could afford to feed them and built houses of paper, scrap wood and tin at the edges of towns and called them "Hoovervilles." They blamed President Hoover for all that had happened to them. One day six-year-old Peggy Ann was playing with a school friend. The friend's mother ran up and yanked Peggy's playmate away, pointing

Lou and the students at the President's School, 1930.

a finger at Peggy Ann and saying, "She is responsible for your father losing his job."

President Hoover urged Congress to fund his construction programs and pass laws to help the people. The Reconstruction Finance Corporation was approved by Congress in 1932, making $2 billion available to rescue failing banks, railroads, factories, homeowners, and farmers. For the first time the United States, government was trying to rescue the American people. But it was too late and not enough.

Lou deeply felt the mounting criticism and blame heaped on Bert. She did everything she could to support his efforts. Entertainment at the White House became simpler. Lou directed a campaign to support the domestic cotton industry and shocked the public by wearing a cotton evening gown to a state function rather than the normal dress made from yards and yards of silk.

Like Bert, Lou felt the key to saving the country was through voluntary efforts of people rather through government relief programs. She believed in *noblesse oblige*—that having wealth obligates one to serve others. In radio broadcasts, Lou said, "The ones who are not in trouble will have to help the ones who are." She asked women to volunteer and help others, insisting that ample food and clothing was available for all, if only people shared. She encouraged children to "be a help to all about you."

Lou set the Girl Scouts on a program of aid. Some donated their weekly dues to purchase milk for babies and bread for bread lines.

Personally, Lou received thousands of pleas for help. She called them "fire alarms." She would try to find assistance through local organizations or through a national organization such as the Red Cross, but if no help could be found, she often provided the help

Lou in the famous cotton dress, April 1932.

herself. She sent checks through an intermediary so she could remain anonymous.

As the Depression grew worse, Lou became more protective of Bert. She walked with him, talking and smoothing his brow. If distance separated them, she sent encouraging telegrams. The public saw Bert as someone who did not care. Lou knew that was not true.

To her friends, Lou confessed how hurt and unhappy she was. But to the public, she presented a gentle, serene face. The public interpreted the Hoovers' reserved ways as uncaring, not realizing the good deeds they were doing. The country became increasingly hostile, and defeat hung over the White House. Allan said it gave him "the willies."

In June 1932, unemployed workers, 90 percent of them World War I veterans, marched on Washington. The Bonus Act of 1924 had given every veteran a certificate that was payable in 1945, but the men, named the "Bonus Army," wanted the money immediately. President Hoover did not believe the nation could afford to pay it at that time.

Crowds of veterans poured into the Capital and camped across the river. They built shacks along Pennsylvania Avenue and occupied condemned buildings west of the White House and on the Mall. A letter to Lou from the executive secretary of the Commission on Church and Social Services told her that many men had brought their families. Lou immediately, and quietly, sent food and blankets.

The men demonstrated daily, but the Senate voted against the bonus bill and instead authorized $100,000 to aid the marchers in returning home. Most of the veterans left Washington, but about two thousand stayed, their anger growing.

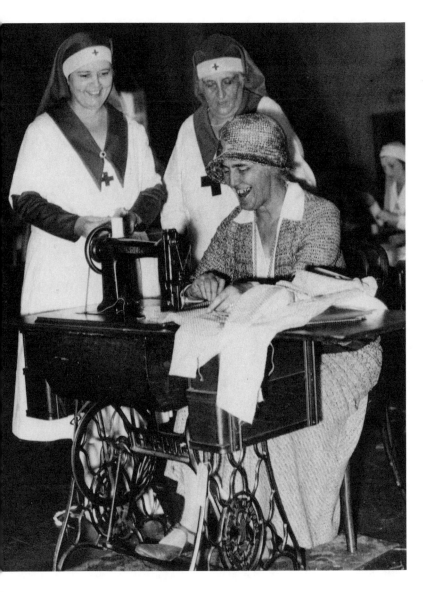

Lou helps the Red Cross sew garments for the unemployed.

General MacArthur used force to drive the Bonus Marchers out of Washington, D.C.

Finally, Bert ordered police to clear the area. The veterans threw bricks at the police; violence ignited. Two demonstrators were killed. Bert ordered Secretary of War Hurley to use federal troops to help, advising him to "use all humanity consistent with the due execution of the law." Women and children were to be evacuated first. Hurley gave the job to the Army chief of staff, Douglas MacArthur.

MacArthur called in a thousand soldiers. The Third Cavalry troops under Major George S. Patton, Jr. drew their sabers and prepared to charge. Six tanks, tear gas, and a machine gun unit made ready. Major Dwight Eisenhower, serving under MacArthur, pleaded with him not to escalate the affair, but MacArthur ignored him. MacArthur also ignored the president. He poured troops into the encampment before the women and children left. Fires sprung up

Lou campaigning from the rear of the Presidential Train, October 1932.

everywhere as the troops drove the "Bonus Army" out.

President Hoover, unaware that his orders had not been obeyed by MacArthur, stated that he was "pleased" the situation had been brought under control. The press accused the president of being insensitive and of not caring about the "little man."

Bert still believed his policies could beat the Depression. He accepted his party's nomination to run for re-election. In Chicago, the Democratic Party nominated Franklin Delano Roosevelt. Roosevelt's campaign speeches accused Hoover of doing nothing to halt the Depression. However, some of Hoover's policies would become the basis of Roosevelt's own program, called the New Deal. Lou listened with anger. She thought Roosevelt's statements were untrue and unfair.

Bert began stumping the country, trying to tell everyone of his fight to save industry, farming, the natural resources. Lou stood by his side, traveling day after day. She tried to smile and make upbeat speeches. They traveled 12,000 miles in six weeks. Bert pointed out that other nations, too, had suffered the end of good times. The economic depression was worldwide.

But people weren't listening. At Detroit loud boos and chants of "Down with Hoover!" filled the air. Crowds of unemployed shoved to the front, shouting at the president. In Chicago, four armed men were arrested at the train station. Bert and Lou drove to their hotel through crowds demanding that the president be hanged. Then, near St. Paul, Minnesota, a man was caught pulling up spikes from the rails over which the Hoover train would pass.

People threw rotten vegetables at the train. In Kansas City tomatoes splashed on Lou and Bert. "I can't go on," Bert said, and

Bert delivered his farewell speech at the Lincoln Day Dinner, February 12, 1933.

Lou put her arm around him. On the last day of the campaign the presidential motorcade drove through silent crowds in San Francisco. But in Palo Alto, "Welcome Home" banners greeted Lou and Bert; a bountiful supper was waiting. Bert was too exhausted to give the speech prepared for his friends. Lou told a Secret Service agent, "We are carrying on." She still felt that Americans surely wouldn't reject Bert after all he had done. The Hoovers cast their ballots in Palo Alto and then waited at their San Juan Hill home for the returns.

By nine o'clock that evening, Bert's presidency had suffered rejection across the nation. Outside, faithful students and friends sang college songs and cheered. "Sis-boom-bah! President and Mrs. Hoover! Rah! Rah! Rah!" But Hoover had been defeated. Fewer than 40 percent of the voters had cast ballots for him. Bert and Lou went out on the terrace to thank their loyal supporters. Then Bert put his arm in Lou's and said, "Good-night, my friends. That's that."

Because of the difficulties of travel in the days of the founding fathers, the new president elected in November didn't take office until March. Bert had asked Congress to enact a law that allowed the president to begin his term in January. A bill was passed into law, but it wouldn't take effect until the next presidency. So Lou and Bert returned to Washington.

They did not hold the traditional New Year's Day reception on January 1, 1933, and the reception was never held again. Bert continued his duties and worked hard to keep the country on course. But the situation grew worse.

To Lou fell the chore of closing Camp Rapidan. She sadly said good-bye to their retreat. There she had been happy, able to be herself and to entertain informally. The fireplace chimneys were stuffed to keep out wintery blasts, and the water pipes were drained. The Hoovers gave the camp to the state of Virginia with the recommendation that it be reserved for succeeding presidents. The camp was transferred to the new Shenandoah National Park in the spring, but no president ever used it again.

At the White House, Lou packed their belongings and picked out gifts of glassware, china, pictures, and other items for the staff. A naval transport shipped their things to San Francisco. Lou invited Eleanor Roosevelt for an informal visit to the White House to help her prepare to move in. The White House began to be fitted for the president-elect with carefully hidden ramps readied for his wheelchair.

On Inauguration Day, Bert and Lou joined Franklin and Eleanor Roosevelt for the ride to Capitol Hill. This time, Lou had no trouble getting to the podium. She listened to "Hail to the Chief" played for her husband for the last time. Then Franklin Delano Roosevelt took the oath of office, and the country had a new president.

When the inauguration ended, the Hoovers rode to Union Station where five thousand people waited for them. "You've done your duty," someone called to Bert, causing him to smile slightly in his bashful way. Girl Scouts presented Lou with candy and roses.

The couple had come to Washington as praised and loved as any president and first lady, but they lost their place in history. Bert left the presidency as one of the least popular men in America. Before the day ended he had received a death threat.

Chapter Nine

Last Years

Back at San Juan Hill, Lou felt as if the healing could begin. She and Bert would finally have time to be together. She loved retirement. Accompanied by her dogs, Pat and Weegie, she hiked and rode her bicycle, or strolled down University Avenue, waving and greeting old friends as she shopped.

Lou remained active. Students from Stanford held meetings on her terraces and shared buffet dinners. She'd often telephone the proctor of Robie Hall and say, "It's a beautiful evening. Bring some girls up to enjoy the view. I have sixty-five cups." With Bert, Lou helped the War Library they'd planned take shape at Stanford. Lou loved being a private citizen again.

She found time to write articles and speak for the causes she believed in. She spoke all over the country on behalf of the 400,000 Girl Scouts, advocating scouting for the handicapped as her special project. Lou believed that a girl with a handicap should be welcomed exactly as every other girl. In 1935, Lou was again elected national president of the Girl Scouts by a unanimous vote.

The Red Cross, the Salvation Army, the Community Chest, and the YWCA all became recipients of Lou's desire to help others. She founded the Friends of Music at Stanford and served as its first chairperson, underwriting several concerts. For an NBC radio series, Lou delivered an address on "What does the future hold for our daughters."

With Allan's help she fulfilled one project close to her heart. They purchased Bert's birthplace at West Branch, Iowa, and restored the house to look as it did when Bert was born. They bought additional land and set up an association to preserve the site permanently. The Hoover Birthplace Society was incorporated.

Overall, Lou was content with their life in California, but Bert felt cut off from world events. He thought about going back into business. But what he really wanted was a call from President Roosevelt, asking him to come back into public service in some way. The call never came. Bert felt he should be in New York, so for most of the year, beginning in 1934, he resided in the Waldorf-Astoria. Lou traveled back and forth to be with him.

On March 17, 1937, Allan married Margaret "Coby" Coberly, and in November 1938, baby Allan Henry Hoover II was born. He was followed in 1940 by Andrew Hoover.

In 1940, Lou and Bert rented a permanent suite, 31-A, at the Waldorf Astoria, and Lou made a home for them the way she'd always done. There she entertained old friends and new ones, inviting people from nearby and far way. She continued to travel back and forth to California.

Lou attended the dedication of an elementary school in Whittier, named the Lou Henry Hoover School. She gave the commencement address to Stanford's graduating class of 1941, speaking as she often did about the pioneering spirit that was always needed. She admitted to the class that she used to stand by the ocean "on the verge of tears because I thought there was nothing left to pioneer into."

The United States entered World War II in December 1941. Bert had warned that another war would come. Lou shared her husband's abhorrence of war because she had seen firsthand in China and Europe the suffering it brought.

Allan and his family moved to a house in Palo Alto, so Lou visited whenever she could. In January 1943, Allan's new daughter was named Lou Henry Hoover.

A year later, in New York, on January 7, 1944, Lou and a friend went to a concert performed by Mildred Dilling, the harpist who had performed as a young artist at the White House. The music brought back many memories. When Lou arrived back at 31-A, Bert, dressed for dinner, was there with their old friend Edgar Rickard. Lou told them she was tired and was going to rest.

A short time later, Bert went in to wake Lou and found her on the floor. He lifted her to the bed and called for a doctor. But within a few minutes Lou died of a heart attack.

Three days later 1,500 mourners filled St. Bartholomew's Episcopal Church. Two hundred Girl Scouts sat in the pews along with many other notable people. A fifty-member choir sang Lou's favorite hymns, among them "Nearer My God to Thee." The chairman of the American Friends Service Committee read from the Bible. Lou had requested that no eulogy be given when it came time for her funeral, and her wishes were respected.

That afternoon Bert and his sons left Grand Central Station with Lou's casket. She was going home to Palo Alto one last time. At the service held in Stanford's Memorial Church, an old friend spoke:

Lou in 1943.

Bert, Herbert, Jr., and Allan at Lou's funeral, January 10, 1944.

"There is no finer example of how to live than was given to us by Lou Henry Hoover."

When Bert began to sort through Lou's personal papers, he found her desk filled with uncashed checks—repayments for aid she'd given to thousands of people.

The year Lou died, Bert sold their house on S Street in Washington. Following Lou's wishes, he presented their home on San Juan Hill as a gift to Stanford to serve as the university president's residence. The home was eventually named the Lou Henry Hoover House. He lived in their Suite 31-A at the Waldorf-Astoria in New York for twenty years after Lou died.

The Girl Scouts set up a tribute to their former leader by establishing criteria for Lou Henry Hoover Memorial Forests and Wildlife

Sanctuaries. The Lou Henry Hoover Memorial Room at the National Girl Scout Camping Center in Maryland was dedicated in 1955. For the dedication, twelve-year-old Lou Henry Hoover II unveiled a portrait of her grandmother.

A new home for the YWCA in Palo Alto was dedicated in 1963 and named the Lou Henry Hoover Memorial Building. At the Hoover Institute on War, Revolution, and Peace at Stanford, there is a Lou Henry Hoover Memorial Room.

When Bert died in 1964, he was buried at West Branch, Iowa, at the Hoover Park that Allan and his mother had established. Lou's remains were moved from Alta Mesa cemetery in Palo Alto to West Branch to join Bert in their final resting place.

From a grassy knoll, their graves overlook the park, the Herbert Hoover Presidential Library and Museum, and the small town where Bert was born.

Timeline

1874 Lou born March 29 in Waterloo, Iowa.

1879 Henry family leaves for a brief stay in Corsicana, Texas.

1883 Sister, Jean, born on June 30 in Waterloo, Iowa.

1887 Henry family moves to Whittier, California, in September.

1893 Lou graduates from San Jose State Normal School and moves home to Monterey, California; works in father's bank.

1894 Lou enters Leland Stanford University; meets Herbert Hoover, Professor Branner's assistant.

1898 Lou receives A.B. degree in geology from Stanford on May 25.

1899 Lou and Bert Hoover marry on February 10. The newlyweds leave for China aboard the *S.S. Coptic* on February 11.

1900 In June the Boxers rise up against all "foreign devils." Lou and Bert leave China and arrive in London on October 1.

1901-1902 Lou lives in Japan while Bert returns to China.

1902 Lou moves with Bert to Kalgoorlie, Australia.

1903 Herbert Hoover, Jr., is born on August 4 in London.

1904-1907 Family travels on Bert's business to Australia, Tasmania, and Cairo, Egypt.

1907 Allan Henry Hoover born July 16 in London.

1907-1912 Hoover family travels to Burma and other places around the world with their "home base" at their Red House in London. Translates *De Re Metallica*, a 16th century mining book written in Latin

1914 Mining and Metallurgical Society of America award Lou and Bert gold medal for translating *De Re Metallica*. Lou becomes president of the Society of American Women. Great Britain and Germany go to war.

1914-1917 In London Lou organizes and chairs Society of American Women's War Relief Committee. Lou speaks in the United States on behalf of Belgians and raises funds for food and clothing.

1917 United States declares war on Germany. Bert is appointed head of Food Administration by President Woodrow Wilson and the Hoovers move to Washington, D.C.

1917-1918 Lou becomes National Commissioner of Girl Scouts of America. She founds a Girl Scout Troop in Palo Alto.

1918-1919 World War I ends. In September King Albert of Belgium confers the Cross of Chevalier, Order of Leopold, on Lou in recognition of her relief work on behalf of Belgium.

1921 Bert becomes Secretary of Commerce under President Harding. Lou becomes National Vice President of the Girl Scouts.

1922 Lou is elected National President of the Girl Scouts. Helps found the National Amateur Athletic Federation.

1923 Lou chairs first National Conference on Athletics and Physical Education for Women and Girls. President Harding dies on August 2.

1925 Lou becomes a National Vice President of GSA.

1926 Lou serves on the building committee of the Washington YWCA in their national campaign to raise $700,000 for a new building in Washington, D.C.

Lou and Bert become grandparents; Peggy Ann Hoover is born to Herbert, Jr., and Margaret on March 18.

1928 Bert is elected President in November.

1929 Lou becomes Honorary President of GSA. Lou is denounced for entertaining Mrs. Oscar DePriest in the White House. The stock market crashes in October.

1929-1930 Lou researches and writes a history of the White House and its furnishings.

1930 The President's School at Dark Hollow opens in February.

1932 The "Bonus Army" descends on Washington, D.C.,demanding early payment of their service bonuses. In November Bert loses presidenchy to Franklin Roosevelt. Lou and Bert return to their home on San Juan Hill to live.

1933 Lou resumes her service work, especially work for the Girl Scouts. She is Honorary Vice-President of the GSA from 1933-1944; National Board Member from 1933-1935.

1934 Bert and Lou divide their time between New York and Palo Alto.

1935 Lou is unanimously elected National President of GSA.

1938 Lou becomes Girl Scout Palo Alto Commissioner.

1941 On December 7 the United States enters World War II. Lou helps Bert with relief efforts for small nations overrun by Nazis.

1944 On January 7 Lou dies in her Waldorf-Astoria apartment.

Bibliography

Primary Sources

Lou Henry Hoover Papers, Hoover Presidential Library, West Branch, Iowa.

Curator's Collection, Hoover Presidential Library, West Branch, Iowa.

Allan Hoover Papers, Hoover Presidential Library, West Branch, Iowa.

Oral History Interview with Alonzo Fields, Hoover Presidential Library, West Branch, Iowa.

Oral History Interview with Marie McSpadden Sands, Hoover Presidential Library, West Branch, Iowa.

Secondary Sources

Books

Anthony, Carl Sferrazza. *First Ladies: The Saga of the Presidents' Wives and their Power, 1789-1961.* New York: William Morrow and Company, Inc., 1990.

Barzman, Sol. *The First Ladies.* New York: Cowles Book Company, Inc., 1970.

Bassett, Margaret. *Profiles & Portraits of American Presidents & Their Wives.* Freeport, Maine: The Bond Wheelwright Company, and New York: Grosset & Dunlap, 1969.

Blumberg, Rhoda. *First Ladies.* New York and London: Franklin Watts, 1977. (Children's book)

Boller, Paul F., Jr. *Presidential Wives.* New York and Oxford: Oxford University Press, 1988.

Brooks, Gertrude Zeth. *First Ladies of the White House.* Chicago, Ill.: Chas. Hallbert & Company, 1969.

Caroli, Betty Boyd. *First Ladies*. New York and Oxford: Oxford University Press, 1987.

Dennis, Ruth. *The Homes of the Hoovers*. West Branch, Iowa: Herbert Hoover Presidential Library Association, Inc., 1986.

Diller, Daniel C., and Stephen L. Robertson._*The Presidents, First Ladies, and Vice Presidents*. Washington, D.C.: Congressional Quarterly, Inc., 1989.

Editors of "Country Beautiful." *Herbert Hoover's Challenge toAmerica: His Life and Words*. Waukesha, Wisconsin: Country Beautiful Foundation, Inc., 1965.

Furman, Bess. *White House Profile: A social history of the White House, its occupants and its festivities*. Indianapolis and New York: The Bobbs-Merrill Company, Inc., 1951.

Gerlinger, Irene Hazard. *Mistresses of the White House*. Freeport, New York: Books for Libraries Press, 1970.

Gutin, Myra G. *The President's Partner: The First Lady in the Twentieth Century*. New York, Westport, Conn. and London: Greenwood Press, 1989.

Hay, Peter. *All the Presidents' Ladies: Anecdotes of the Women Behind the Men in the White House*. New York: Viking Penguin, Inc., 1988.

Hilton, Suzanne. *The World of Young Herbert Hoover*. New York: Walker and Company, 1987.

Hoover, Herbert. *The Memoirs of Herbert Hoover: Years of Adventure, 1874-1920*. New York: The Macmillan Company, 1951.

Hoover, Herbert C. *Principles of Mining: Valuation, Organization and Administration*. New York: McGraw-Hill Book Company, Inc., and London: Hill Publishing Co., Ltd., 1909.

Hoover, Irwin H. "Ike." *Forty-two Years in the White House*. Boston: Houghton-Mifflin, 1934.

Jefferies, Ona Griffin. *In and Out of the White House*. New York: Wilfred Funk, Inc., 1960.

Klapthor, Margaret Brown. *The First Ladies*. Washington, D.C.: White House Historical Association with cooperation of National Geographic Society, 1975.

Kurtz, Alice K. *Lou Henry Hoover: The Independent Girl: A Curriculum Guide*. West Branch, Iowa: Herbert Hoover Presidential Library, 1994.

Mayer, Dale C., ed. *Lou Henry Hoover: Essays on a Busy Life.* Worland, Wyoming: High Plains Publishing Company, Inc., 1994.

McLean, Hulda Hoover. *Genealogy of the Herbert Hoover Family.* Stanford, California: The Hoover Institution on War, Revolution, and Peace, 1967.

Melick, Arden Davis. *Wives of the Presidents.* Maplewood, New Jersey: Hamond Incorporated, 1972.

Myers, William Starr, and Walter H. Newton. *The Hoover Administration: A Documented Narrative.* New York: Charles Scribner's Sons, and London: Charles Scribner's Sons, Ltd., 1936.

Nash, George H. *The Life of Herbert Hoover: The Engineer, 1874-1914.* New York and London: W. W. Norton & Company, 1983.

Nash, George H. *The Life of Herbert Hoover: The Humanitarian, 1914-1917.* New York and London: W. W. Norton & Company, 1988.

Nye, Frank T., Jr. *Doors of Opportunity: The Life and Legacy of Herbert Hoover.* West Branch, Iowa: Herbert Hoover Presidential Library Association, Inc., 1988.

Parks, Lillian Rogers. *My Thirty Years Backstairs at the White House.* New York: Fleet Publishing Corp., 1961.

Pryor, Helen B. *Lou Henry Hoover: Gallant First Lady.* New York: Dodd, Mead & Company, 1969.

Quinn Sandra L., and Sanford Kanter. *America's Royalty: All the Presidents' Children.* Westport, Conn. and London: Greenwood Press, 1983.

Randolph, Mary. *Presidents and First Ladies.* New York: D. Appleton-Century Company, Inc., 1936.

Riley, Glenda. *Cities on the Cedar: A Portrait of Cedar Falls, Waterloo, and Black Hawk County.* Parkersburg, Iowa: Mid-Prairie Books, 1988.

Rosebush, James S. *First Lady: Public Wife.* Lanham, Maryland: Madison Books, 1987.

Schwieder, Dorothy, Thomas Morain, and Lynn Nielsen. *Iowa Past to Present: The People and the Prairie.* Ames, Iowa: Iowa State University Press, 1989.

Scott, Mel. *The San Francisco Bay Area: A Metropolitan Perspective.* Berkley and Los Angeles: University of California, 1959.

Smith, Richard Norton. *An Uncommon Man: The Triumph of Herbert Hoover*. New York: Simon and Schuster, 1984.

Smith, Richard Norton. *Mrs. President: Biographical Sketches from Martha to Barbara*. West Branch, Iowa: Herbert Hoover Presidential Library, 1990.

Tebbel, John, and Sarah Miles Watts. *The Press and the Presidency: From George Washington to Ronald Regan*. New York and Oxford: Oxford University Press, 1985.

Truman, Margaret. *First Ladies*. New York: Random House, 1995.

Truman, Margaret. *White House Pets*. New York: David McKay Company, Inc., 1969.

Waldrup, Carole Chandler. *Presidents' Wives: The Lives of 44 American Women of Strength*. Jefferson, North Carolina, and London: McFarland & Company, Inc., 1989.

Wall, Joseph Frazier. *Iowa: A Bicentennial History*. New York: Norton & Company, Inc. and Nashville, Tenn.: American Association for State and Local History, 1978.

Wilbur, Ray Lyman, and Arthur Mastick Hyde. *The Hoover Policies*. New York: Charles Scribner's Sons, 1937.

Wilson, Joan Hoff. *Herbert Hoover: Forgotten Progressive*. Boston and Toronto: Little, Brown and Company, 1975.

Articles

Burke, Frank G. "Prologue in Perspective: First Ladies as National Leaders," *Prologue*. vol. 19 (Summer '87), p. 68-69.

Cherry-Hoffman, Stephanie. "Lou Henry Hoover: The Life of a Dynamic American Woman," *The American Road*. Volume 10, Number 1, Summer 1985.

Day, David S. "A New Perspective on the `DePriest Tea' Historiographic Controversy: Mrs. Lou Henry Hoover's Papers," *The Journal of Negro History*. Vol. 75 (Summer/Fall '90) p. 120-4.

Gould, Lewis L. "Modern First Ladies: An Institutional Perspective," *Prologue*. Vol. 19 (Summer '87) p. 71-83.

"Hoover granddaughter, Iowa First Lady open new First Ladies exhibit," *The American Road*. Volume 15, Number 2, Spring 1990, p. 5.

"Hoover Tower galleries to be overhauled," *The American Road*. Volume 15, Number 2, Spring 1990, p. 9.

"'Lou' wows Washington!!!" *The American Road*. Volume 15, Number 2, Spring 1990, p. 4.

Melville, J. Keith. "The First Lady and the Cowgirl," *Pacific Historical Review*. Vol. 57 (Feb. '88) p. 73-6.

Mayer, Dale C. "Not One to Stay at Home: The Papers of Lou Henry Hoover," *Prologue*. vol. 19, (Summer '87) p. 85-93.

Mayer, Dale C. "An Uncommon Woman: The Quiet Leadership Style of Lou Henry Hoover," *Presidential Studies Quarterly*. Volume XX, Number 4, Fall 1990, p. 685-698.

Reference Books

"Australia," *World Book Encyclopedia*, Vol. 1, p. 750-67.

"Belgium," *World Book Encyclopedia*, Vol. 2, p. 178-84

"Burma," *World Book Encyclopedia*, Vol.2, p. 594-98.

"California," *World Book Encyclopedia*, Vol. 3, p. 32-53.

"China," *World Book Encyclopedia*, Vol. 3, p. 376-91.

"Depression," *World Book Encyclopedia*, Vol. 4, p. 125-26.

"Hoover, Herbert Clark," *World Book Encyclopedia*, Vol. 8, p. 292-97.

"Hoover, Herbert Clark, Jr.," *World Book Encyclopedia*, Vol. 8, p. 298.

"Hoover Dam," *World Book Encyclopedia*, Vol. 8, p. 298-99.

"Iowa," *World Book Encyclopedia*, Vol. 9, p. 300-14.

"Los Angeles," *World Book Encyclopedia*, Vol. 11, p. 404-11.

"President of the United States," *World Book Encyclopedia*, Vol. 14, p. 676-82.

"Railroad," *World Book Encyclopedia*, Vol. 15, p. 102-17.

"San Francisco," *World Book Encyclopedia*, Vol. 16, p. 86-9.

"Stanford," *World Book Encyclopedia*, Vol. 16, p. 657.

"United States, History of," *World Book Encyclopedia*, Vol. 18, p. 86-120.

"White House," *World Book Encyclopedia*, Vol. 19, p. 240-44.

"World War I," *World Book Encyclopedia*, Vol. 19, p. 364-79.

"The Man Who Served Mankind," *World Book Encyclopedia: Year Book 1965*. p. 300.

"Herbert Hoover Memorial," *World Book Encyclopedia: Year Book 1973*. p. 415.

Drama

Christian, Rebecca. *First Lady Lou*. Iowa City, Iowa: The Riverside Theatre, 1988.

Index

J
B
HOOVER

Colbert, Nancy A.

Lou Henry Hoover.

$18.95   Grades 7-9

DATE